SOCCER'S Greatest Clubs

AC Milan

Kevin Snow

Cavendish Square
New York

Published in 2021 by Cavendish Square Publishing, LLC
243 5th Avenue, Suite 136, New York, NY 10016

First Edition

Library of Congress Cataloging-in-Publication Data

Names: Snow, Kevin, author. | Cavendish Square Publishing LLC.
Title: AC Milan / Kevin Snow.
Other titles: AC (Milan, Italy)
Description: First Edition. | New York : Cavendish Square, 2021. | Series: Soccer's greatest clubs | Includes bibliographical references and index.
Identifiers: LCCN 2019040285 (print) | LCCN 2019040286 (ebook) | ISBN 9781502652744 (Library Binding) | ISBN 9781502652737 (Paperback) | ISBN 9781502652751 (eBook)
Subjects: LCSH: Milan (Soccer team)--History--Juvenile literature. | Società moderna e contemporanea. Analisi e contributi | Soccer teams--Italy--Milan--Juvenile literature.
Classification: LCC GV943.6.M54 S66 2021 (print) | LCC GV943.6.M54 (ebook) | DDC 796.3340945/211--dc23
LC record available at https://lccn.loc.gov/2019040285
LC ebook record available at https://lccn.loc.gov/2019040286

Editor: Kristen Susienka
Copy Editor: Rebecca Rohan
Designer: Joe Parenteau

The photographs in this book are used by permission and through the courtesy of: Cover Giuseppe Cottini/NurPhoto via Getty Images; series art (badge) Onur Cem/Shutterstock.com; series art (field) comzeal images/Shutterstock.com; series art (soccer ball) FocusStocker/Shutterstock.com; series art (crowd silhouette) Nosyrevy/Shutterstock.com; pp. 4, 8, 34 Paolo Bona/Shutterstock.com; p. 6 Grazia Neri/ALLSPORT/Getty Images; p. 9 Dino Panato/Getty Images; p. 10 Marco Luzzani/Getty Images; p. 12 The History Collection/Alamy Stock Photo; p. 14 MARKA/Alamy Stock Photo; p. 16 Hum Images/Alamy Stock Photo; p. 17 © iStockphoto.com/fightbegin; p. 20 Historic Collection/Alamy Stock Photo; p. 23 Philippe Bouchon/AFP/Getty Images; p. 25 Tony Marshall/PA Images/Alamy Stock Photo; pp. 26, 28 Fabio Diena/Shutterstock.com; p. 30 Jamie McDonald/Getty Images; p. 31 Fabrizio Andrea Bertani/Shutterstock.com; p. 38 Maurizio Borsari/Nippon News/Aflo Co. Ltd./Alamy Stock Photo; p. 42 Mike Hewitt/Getty Images; p. 43 Enrico Locci/Getty Images; p. 44 Ben Radford/Getty Images; p. 46 Giuseppe Cacace/AFP/Getty Images; p. 49 Kazuhiro Nogi/AFP via Getty Images; p. 50 Marco Bertorello/AFP/Getty Images; p. 53 bestino/Shutterstock.com.

CPSIA compliance information: Batch #CS20CSQ For further information contact Cavendish Square Publishing LLC, New York, New York, at 1-877-980-4450.

Printed in the United States of America

TABLE OF CONTENTS

Chapter 1:
Soccer and AC Milan. 5

Chapter 2:
Who Is AC Milan? 13

Chapter 3:
Good Games, Awards, and Trophies . . .27

Chapter 4:
Tough Times 35

Chapter 5:
Looking to the Future 47

Chronology 54

Glossary 56

Further Information 58

Selected Bibliography 60

Index. 62

About the Author 64

Members of AC Milan celebrate a goal at home in Milan in 2005.

1

SOCCER AND AC MILAN

There's no question that soccer is the most popular sport in the world. A 2018 study called the *World Football Report* said that more than 40 percent of the world's population is interested in the game of soccer. What makes soccer so special? Some people say it's because anyone can play it. You also don't need to buy a lot of expensive equipment. Games don't always have to be played on a special field. Soccer can be played in your backyard, on the street, or even at the beach. All you need to get started is a soccer ball.

THE GAME OF SOCCER

An official soccer game has 11 players on each team, including the goalkeeper, or goalie. Games are normally played on a grassy field, called a pitch, with official lines and markings as the boundaries. Each team guards half of the field. The players move the ball down the field by kicking it to the other team's half and putting the ball in the net. That's called a goal. The team that scores the most goals is the winner.

The goalie is the player who protects the net. One of the rules of soccer is that a goalie must wear a different-colored jersey than the rest of the team. This is to help the referee see the goalie better during games. Goalkeepers also wear gloves and are the only player on the field allowed to touch the ball with his or her hands.

Goaltender Sebastiano Rossi, who played 12 seasons with AC Milan, stops a penalty shot during a 2001 game.

The games are divided into two timed sections, or halves. Teams switch ends, or sides, at the end of the first half. Game times can be different lengths. A professional soccer game is 90 minutes long. This means that each half lasts 45 minutes. Sometimes games run a little bit longer if there's been a lot of pauses in play. The teams play longer to make up the time. At the end of the second half, if the teams have the same amount of goals, they will play an additional period called "extra time." Extra time lasts 30 minutes and is divided into 2 separate 15-minute halves. The team that scores more goals than the other at the end of extra time is the winner.

If neither team scores in extra time, a penalty shootout will then take place. This means that one player from each team will shoot the ball at the goal from a spot in front of the goal. The other team's goalie tries to stop the ball. The teams will take turns doing this until one has more goals than the other. Some of the most exciting and dramatic moments in soccer history have been in penalty shootouts!

THE PRIDE OF MILAN

In much of the world, soccer is called "football." Canada, the United States, and Australia are the main countries that don't call it football. Soccer is a popular sport in Europe. One country with many good soccer teams is Italy. Soccer is Italy's national sport.

A writer on the website LifeInItaly.com tried to explain what soccer means to Italians: "Soccer in Italy is something more than just passion, soccer for Italians means tradition. It's one of the most significant symbols our country has to offer: just like Ferrari, the Coliseum or food. Soccer is also faith, loving your own team means stitching its jersey forever in your heart."

SPORT SHORT

Milan is Italy's most populated city. It has about 3.1 million residents.

AC Milan hosted powerhouse Juventus in this 2014 Serie A game. The two teams are longtime Italian League rivals.

One of the most popular teams in Italy is AC Milan. Their official name is Associazione Calcio Milan and they started playing in 1899. *Calcio* means "football" or "soccer" in Italian.

AC Milan is a club team that plays in the highest level of Italian professional soccer, called Serie A. Serie A is a soccer league, or group of soccer teams that play each other every year. Other top teams in Serie A are Juventus, Inter Milan, Napoli, and Roma. AC Milan plays its home games at San Siro Stadium in Milan.

AC Milan has won 18 championships, or league titles, in Serie A as of 2019. This means they've finished in first place in Serie A 18 times. As of 2019, Juventus FC has the most Serie A titles in league history, with 35.

ITALY'S SERIE LEAGUES

The Serie A league is the highest level of professional soccer in Italy. The league started in the 1929–1930 season. It's one of the best leagues in Europe. Serie A is a national league. Teams compete from all over Italy. There are 20 teams in the league as of 2020.

Serie B is the second-highest level in Italy. It's also a national league, and in the 2019–2020 season, it had 20 teams. The third level of Italian professional soccer is called Serie C.

Teams in Serie A play a total of 38 games each season. Teams get three points for a win, one for a tie (also called a draw), and zero for a loss. The team that has the most points at the end of the season wins the league title, called the scudetto.

The celebration following AC Milan's win of the 2010–2011 Serie A championship was filled with happiness and cheering. What made it even better was that the win was in front of the team's home fans.

COLORS OF MILAN

Red and black have been the main colors of AC Milan since the team started in 1899. The powerful colors have also given the team its Italian nickname, "Rossoneri." This means the "red and blacks." The team has also been called "Il Diavolo," or "the Devil."

Midfielder Hakan Calhanoglu wears the iconic black and red AC Milan jersey.

The Serie A season runs from August to May. The teams play each other twice, once at home and once on the road (or away).

The teams that finish in the last three spots in Serie A are dropped (or relegated) to Serie B for the next season. They are replaced in Serie A by the top three teams in Serie B, who move up (or are promoted) for the following season.

SPORT SHORT

Novelist Ernest Hemingway and legendary dancer/actor Fred Astaire were both born in 1899, the same year AC Milan started.

THE CHAMPIONS LEAGUE

The first- and second-place teams each season in Serie A receive an automatic spot in the playoffs of an inter-European competition called the UEFA Champions League. UEFA stands for the Union of European Football Associations. It's a European soccer group. Many of the best teams play in the Champions League. The third-place team in Serie A can try to gain a spot in the Champions League playoffs by playing more games.

The UEFA Champions League is a yearly tournament that includes all of the best club teams from the top leagues in Europe. It's one of the best tournaments held each year. It was started in 1955 as the European Cup and renamed as the Champions League in 1992.

AC Milan has done very well in European club tournaments. They have won seven European Cup/Champions League titles as of late 2019. This is the most of any team in Italian soccer and second-most in Europe. Only Spanish team Real Madrid has won more European Cup/Champions League titles.

Englishman Herbert Kilpin, shown here, was one of the men who started AC Milan in 1899.

2

WHO IS AC MILAN?

In December 1899, a group of English immigrants in Italy started the team we now know as AC Milan. Two of the main people who began the group were Alfred Edwards and Herbert Kilpin.

Herbert Kilpin moved to Turin, Italy, in 1891. Alfred Edwards moved to Milan in 1899. Kilpin worked for Edoardo Bosio, who owned a factory. Bosio started Internazionale Torino, which is considered to be the first Italian soccer club. Kilpin played some games for Torino and became the first player from England to play soccer in another country for a professional team. Edwards was a wealthy businessman and a sports fan.

FORMING A TEAM

Kilpin had met Edwards before at one of the soccer games he hosted. The two men were both out with friends at a restaurant one night when they saw each other again and started talking. Soon, the conversation moved to soccer. The men agreed to start the Milan Foot-Ball and Cricket Club. Cricket is a popular sport that started in England. Games are played between two teams of 11 players. It takes place on a grass field. Players use a wooden bat and a ball with raised leather seams.

Edwards became the first team chairman and president of the club. He had this job until 1909, when he moved back to England. Kilpin was the team's first coach, and he also played and was the team captain, or lead player for the team. He chose the team colors, red and black. When asked why, he said, "We are a team of devils. Our colors are red as fire and black to invoke [bring out] fear in our opponents."

THE FIRST GAME

The Milan Foot-Ball Club played its first Italian League game on April 23, 1901, against a team called Mediolanum. They won the game 2–0. The team had four Italian players and six English players, including Kilpin and his friends.

By the early 1900s, soccer was so popular in Italy that the country formed a national team. Members played their first-ever national game in Milan on May 15, 1910. They defeated France 6–2.

Milan would win the league title in 1901 by winning all three games they played. They defeated the team from Genoa in the championship to win their first title as Italian champions. They would add two more titles in 1906 and 1907.

Herbert Kilpin is still considered a hero in Milan for helping start the team in 1899, and for helping them win their first three league titles. However, he disappeared from the public eye after he stopped playing soccer in 1908. He died in 1916 at age 46. When AC Milan celebrated its 100th anniversary in 1999, the team paid for Kilpin to have a new tombstone in the Monumental Graveyard, one of the two largest cemeteries in Milan.

THE NAME GAME

After starting out as the Milan Foot-Ball and Cricket Club in 1899, the official name of the team was changed a few times in the years following. In 1919, they dropped "cricket" from the team name and also kept the English spelling of Milan (rather than the Italian name, Milano). The reason for keeping the English spelling was out of respect for the Englishmen who helped create the team. The name was changed again in 1939, this time to Associazione Calcio Milano. This change happened because Italy was run by Benito Mussolini from 1922 to 1943. Mussolini was a dictator, and he tried to control how people thought and acted. He demanded the name to be in Italian only. Once World War II ended and Mussolini's government was defeated, the team's city name was once again changed back to Milan. The team is now known worldwide as AC Milan, or simply, Milan.

SPLITTING UP

AC Milan won Italian League Prima Categoria titles in 1906 and 1907. The Prima Categoria was Italy's top level of soccer until Serie A started. However, AC Milan didn't take part in the 1907–1908 Prima Categoria season. They and other teams didn't like how some teams were using more foreign players than Italian players. To let people know they were unhappy, they decided to boycott the season. This meant they decided not to have their team play because they disagreed with what the other teams were doing.

This disagreement led to a split of AC Milan. A group of people running the team wanted to include more foreign players, while another wanted to be mostly Italian. In March 1908, the group that wanted to include more foreign players left to start a new team in

AC Milan's Gunnar Nordahl (*center*) scores a goal against Inter Milan in 1951.

Milan called Foot-Ball Club Internazionale. The name Internazionale (meaning "international") highlighted their decision to include players from outside Italy, not just Italian players. Internazionale won their first title in 1910. This team still exists today and is known as Internazionale, Inter Milan, or just Inter.

SAN SIRO

AC Milan plays its home games at a stadium called San Siro. They have played there since the stadium was built for the start of the 1926–1927 season. The stadium was originally called the Nuovo Stadio Calcistico San Siro, which translates to San Siro New Football Stadium. It is now known simply as San Siro. It's called San Siro because that's the area of Milan where the stadium is located.

San Siro was a gift from Piero Pirelli, AC Milan's team president from 1909 to 1929. Pirelli paid for the entire

Shown here is San Siro stadium.

SPORT SHORT

San Siro Stadium was officially renamed Giuseppe Meazza Stadium in 1980. Most people still refer to it as San Siro.

project. Construction took 14 months to complete. The team had been playing at Campo di Viale Lombardia for the six years before San Siro. Pirelli wanted to move them to a bigger field that could hold more fans.

San Siro was designed to be a soccer-only stadium, with seating on all four sides that formed a rectangle around the playing field. Pirelli wanted the stadium to look like the ones in England, with fans seated closer to the field. San Siro held 35,000 fans when it first opened.

Some updates have been done over the years, and San Siro now has more than 80,000 seats and a roof to protect players and fans from bad weather. It's the largest Serie A stadium in Italy.

SHARING WITH INTER

AC Milan owned San Siro until 1935, when they sold it to the city of Milan. Today, the team shares the stadium with Inter Milan, the other Serie A team based in Milan. Inter needed a place to play, and the city owners allowed them to move to San Siro in 1947. The two teams have shared it ever since.

Sharing a stadium isn't as difficult as it may seem. Milan and Inter each have separate locker rooms and never play home games on the same day. However, sharing the same home stadium adds some excitement to their yearly derby games. A derby is a game that takes place against rival teams from the same city.

HOW SWEDE IT IS

In the early years of Serie A, Italian players made up the majority of each team's players. The popularity of soccer all over Italy made it easy for teams to find good players. This changed after World War II. Italy was one of the areas that suffered the most in the war. Many good players lost their lives. In order to have a competitive team, coaches were encouraged to look at other European countries for new talent. The first player not from Italy to make a big impact at AC Milan was a Swedish striker, or forward, named Gunnar Nordahl. When he joined Milan in January 1949, Nordahl became the first Swedish player to leave his country to play professionally.

There were some people who wondered if Nordahl would be successful in the Serie A league. It was very competitive. However, he convinced them quickly that he could compete. Nordahl scored 16 goals in 15 games during his first season and became a fan favorite. The adoring Milan fans gave Nordahl nicknames such as "Il Cannoniere" (The Gunner) and "La Pompierone" (The Big Fireman), because he used to work as a fireman in Sweden.

Nordahl's size and skill made him difficult for other teams to defend against. A 7–1 win over Juventus in 1950 saw Nordahl scoring twice. "It was impossible to stop him," Juventus defender Carlo Parola said after the game. "I tried in every possible manner. It was a nightmare for me and my team."

Nordahl played with Milan until 1956 and led Serie A in goals during five of his eight seasons. Nordahl's 221 career goals remain the most in team history as of 2019. He's a member of the AC Milan Hall of Fame and is considered to be one of the greatest Swedish players of all time.

THE GRE-NO-LI

During his first season, Nordahl convinced Milan's management to sign two more Swedish players:

Swedish stars Gunnar Gren (*left*), Gunnar Nordahl (*center*), and Nils Liedholm (*right*) were fan favorites when they played for AC Milan in the 1950s.

Nils Liedholm and Gunnar Gren. The three had played together on Sweden's Olympic team. Nordahl thought they would help Milan win their first Serie A title.

Liedholm and Gren both joined the team for the 1949–1950 season. The two players teamed up with Nordahl to lead AC Milan to a second-place finish and 27 wins. The team also scored 118 goals in 38 games. Nordahl, Gren, and Liedholm combined to score 71 of those goals.

The three players became known as "Gre-No-Li." An Italian journalist that covered the team was having trouble spelling the names of its new players. He decided to shorten their three names into one, and "Gre-No-Li" instantly became part of AC Milan history. Jim Hart of *These Football Times* wrote in 2015: "The Gre-No-Li trio was the tonic that AC Milan needed to build a legacy of success for the northern giants."

AC Milan finally reached the top of Serie A in 1950–1951 when they won their first title. Nordahl led the league in scoring with 34 goals, with most of the assists coming from Gren and Liedholm. AC Milan finished the season with 26 wins and 8 ties in 38 games. They were one point ahead of their rivals, Inter Milan. It was also AC Milan's first Italian championship since the 1906–1907 season. This would be the only title for Gren. He left after the 1952–1953 season.

SPORT SHORT

As of 2019, the AC Milan team record for most goals scored in one Serie A game is nine, against Palermo in 1951.

THE DERBY DELLA MADONNINA

Each season, AC Milan plays a pair of highly anticipated Serie A league games against their local rivals, Inter Milan. These games are part of the annual Derby della Madonnina, or the Milan Derby. Madonnina refers to the gold statue of the Virgin Mary that sits on top of the Milan Cathedral, the fourth-largest church in the world. Milan and Inter share Milan's San Siro Stadium as their home field. This makes their derby more intense than most. The first official game in the derby was played in 1909 with AC Milan winning 3–2. The two teams have also played against each other in various other competitions over the years, and those games are included in the all-time derby results. In 223 games as of late 2019, Inter has 80 wins to Milan's 76. There have also been 67 ties.

Liedholm played his entire professional career, from 1949 to 1961, with Milan. He teamed up with Nordahl to win another Serie A title in 1954–1955. After Nordahl and Gren had both gone, Liedholm was part of two more Serie A championships with Milan, in 1956–1957 and 1958–1959. Liedholm went on to become a successful manager (or coach) and led Milan to their 10th Serie A title in 1978–1979.

AC Milan would win two more Serie A titles in the 1960s, but only one in each of the 1970s and 1980s. In other competitions, they also had success. For example, they captured the European Cup title in 1963 and again in 1969. The European Cup was the previous name of what's now known as the UEFA Champions League. It was called the European Cup from 1955 to 1991. The yearly tournament features the top club teams from across Europe.

ENTER BERLUSCONI

The team was given a new life in February 1986 when Silvio Berlusconi bought AC Milan and became team president. It was his goal to make AC Milan the best team in the world.

Berlusconi made big moves right away. Before the 1987–1988 season, he hired coach Arrigo Sacchi and signed Dutch superstars Ruud Gullit, Marco van Basten, and Frank Rijkaard. They joined a team that already included Italian soccer celebrities Paolo Maldini and Franco Baresi. Those moves helped AC Milan win the 1987–1988 Serie A title, their first in

Silvio Berlusconi is shown here at a press conference in 1986, the year he bought AC Milan.

nine years. The team lost just two games all season and also qualified for the 1989 European Cup. AC Milan advanced to the championship game, where they defeated Romanian team Steaua Bucharest for their first European Cup title in 20 years.

A third-place Serie A finish in 1988–1989 earned AC Milan another trip to the 1990 European Cup tournament. Milan defeated Benfica from Portugal 1–0 in the championship game. The back-to-back European Cup titles also earned this AC Milan team the nickname of "The Immortals." AC Milan then added Champions League titles in 1994, 2003, and 2007. The team has also won the UEFA Super Cup five times as of 2019: 1989, 1990, 1994, 2003, and 2007. This is a one-game event with the winner of the UEFA Champions League playing the winner of the UEFA Europa League. These are Europe's top two club competitions.

THE INVINCIBLES

AC Milan took their game to an entirely new level under new coach Fabio Capello in 1991. They won three straight Serie A titles in 1991–1992, 1992–1993 and 1993–1994, earning them the nickname"The Invincibles."

In 1991–1992, AC Milan became the first team in Serie A history to win the scudetto by not losing a game all season. They won 22 games and had 12 ties to finish 8 points ahead of Juventus.

Their perfect season was also the start of an incredible 58-game streak during which they didn't lose a game. The streak started on May 26, 1991, and ended April 17, 1993, with a 3–1 loss to Juventus.

SPOTLIGHT ON ARRIGO SACCHI

Arrigo Sacchi brought a new flavor of coaching to the club that brought the team success.

Arrigo Sacchi managed AC Milan from 1987 to 1991, and again for the 1996–1997 season. Sacchi didn't get his first coaching job until he was 26 and worked part-time as a shoe salesman to earn extra money.

Sacchi was a creative teacher who had been coaching Parma in Italy's Serie C league when he caught the attention of Milan owner Silvio Berlusconi. Parma defeated Milan twice in a competition called Coppa Italia (Italian Cup), and Sacchi was hired the next season.

However, at first, Sacchi wasn't liked by many fans and media because he'd never played professional soccer. Lots of other coaches played with a team and then went into coaching. Sacchi answered the people who were upset by saying, "I never realized that in order to become a jockey you have to have been a horse first."

AC Milan won the Serie A title in Sacchi's first season, and they captured European Cup championships in 1989 and 1990. Sacchi is now considered one of the game's greatest coaches.

AC Milan captain Massimo Ambrosini accepts the 2010–2011 Serie A trophy, recognizing Milan as league champions.

3

GOOD GAMES, AWARDS, AND TROPHIES

AC Milan's success over the years is highlighted by their many Italian Serie A scudettos and Champions League titles. They've also won five Coppa Italia titles and seven Supercoppa Italiana championships as of 2019, but having won just two Serie A titles since 2004, AC Milan is now taking steps to rebuild its once proud image and make a return to both Italian and European success.

THE LAST SERIE A WIN

After winning their 17th scudetto in 2003–2004, AC Milan didn't win the Serie A league title again until 2010–2011. This victory was very satisfying though, because it stopped AC Milan's rivals, Inter Milan, from winning a sixth title in a row.

AC Milan finished the 2010–2011 season with 24 wins, 10 ties, and 4 losses for a total of 82 points. This placed them six points ahead of the defending champs from Inter. They also defeated Inter in both of their games that season, part of the yearly Derby della Madonnina games. On the defensive side of the ball,

Kaká (*right*) avoids a Liverpool defender in the 2007 UEFA Champions League final.

team to its 17th scudetto. Other players from AC Milan who have received the Ballon d'Or award are George Weah (1995) and Ruud Gullit (1987).

MALDINI'S LEGACY

It's only fitting that defender Paolo Maldini spent his entire career with AC Milan. The Milan native played his first game with the team on January 20, 1985, and retired from soccer at the end of the 2008–2009 season.

Maldini actually started with AC Milan as a 10-year-old in the team's youth program. This is where younger players can go to learn how to play the game of soccer if they have dreams of playing for the professional team when they get older. Some of his youth teammates included future stars Franco Baresi and Alessandro Costacurta.

AC MILAN WOMEN'S TEAM

Members of AC Milan's women's team pose for a picture before a game against Inter Milan in 2019.

AC Milan started a women's professional team in 2018. Former Italian soccer star Carolina Morace became its first coach and got players to join. The team is called AC Milan Women.

The team made its Serie A debut in the 2018–2019 season, finishing in third place overall. The team won 14 games, lost 2, and had 3 ties. Valentina Giacinti was the league's top scorer, with 21 goals. Her teammate, Daniela Sabatino, was second with 17 goals.

Just like the men's league, Serie A is the top league in Italian women's soccer. The women's Serie A league was started in 1968. There were 12 teams in Serie A during the 2018–2019 season, with the top 2 teams each season qualifying to compete in the annual UEFA Women's Champions League. The Women's Champions League was started in 2001 and was known as the Women's Cup until 2009.

Because AC Milan Women is so new, the team has plenty of room to grow and find its place in the league. However, the team's start seems promising, and it has given fans the first taste of an exciting new chapter in women's soccer.

Maldini won the Serie A Defender of the Year award in 2004 and finished third in balloting for the Ballon d'Or in 1994 and 2003. That's unique because voting for that award is normally dominated by goal scorers. In 1995, Maldini finished second for FIFA World Player of the Year.

Tom Sheen of the *Sun* wrote in 2018:

> *His handsome looks, flowing locks, and easy style of play all helped create a mystique around the AC Milan and Italy legend who has gone down as, arguably, the greatest defender ever. Maldini was the complete player, quick, tall, strong, and brilliant on the ball with both feet, but his brain—his ability to spot danger before it happened and his ice cool composure—was his greatest strength.*

Maldini won seven Serie A scudettos with AC Milan, along with five European Cup/Champions League titles. His 647 Serie A appearances are the most in league history, and his combined 902 appearances in Serie A and European games are the most all time for AC Milan as of late 2019.

In August 2018, Maldini returned to AC Milan in a new management job. As of June 2019, he is the team's technical director, responsible for sporting strategy and development, as he tries to help return AC Milan to a place of glory.

FONDAZIONE MILAN

The Fondazione Milan (Milan Foundation) was founded in 2003 to help support the local community through various projects and outreach efforts. It's part of the AC Milan club. The foundation has been involved in more than 100 projects and fundraising efforts since it launched. It has raised nearly €10 million (euros), which is more than $11 million in US dollars.

Many of the foundation's projects revolve around all sports, not just soccer. The foundation uses sports to teach participants values and life lessons. The ultimate goal is to have children and adults of all ages taking part in sports together. They don't want people thinking they can't play sports because of physical disabilities or lack of money.

In the spring of 2019, Fondazione Milan partnered with a local group called PlayMore! to launch the Sport4All initiative. A news story on the Fondazione Milan website explained that the goal of Sport4All is "to promote the practice of sports among people with disabilities together with children, young people and able-bodied adults, and it aims at breaking down all barriers and prejudices."

AC Milan fans show their support during a 2010 game.

4 TOUGH TIMES

Professional sports teams always face challenges. The challenges that fans see are normally just what happens on the field during games. These challenges can include facing a better team, dealing with injuries, or having to play a game in bad weather. It's up to the coaches and players to overcome them to try and win each game they play. However, there are also challenges fans don't see that can affect a team. These are events that happen off the field or behind the scenes. Just because it doesn't happen during a game doesn't mean the players aren't bothered by it. AC Milan has been around for more than 100 years and has faced many challenges. In each case, they've done a very good job of fixing the problems and making the team better.

DEALING WITH SCANDAL

AC Milan's reputation on the field has twice been damaged by major scandals that affected the Italian soccer world. A scandal is an event that involves a person or people doing something that's wrong or

SPORT SHORT

In 2011, 16-year-old Bryan Cristante became the youngest AC Milan player to play in a Champions League game.

illegal. In most cases, a scandal involves people with a lot of money and power over a situation.

The first Milan scandal happened in 1980. It was called *totonero*. This scandal was about gambling and soccer games. When people take part in sports gambling, they spend money to try and predict which team will win or lose each game. If they guess right, they will win more money.

Italians can try to win money legally using *totalcalcio*, a type of sports lottery that is approved by the government. However, *totonero* refers to a form of illegal gambling that isn't approved by the government. *Totonero* gambling normally is on just one or two games at a time, while *totalcalcio* could be on several games.

The most scandalous part of *totonero* involved "match fixing." This is when certain players are paid lots of money to help decide the final score in their games. In 1980, this scandal involved many people. When the police became involved, their investigation found that 30 players took money from Italian businessmen to help "fix" the results of the games. In some cases, the players even bet money against their own team.

In his book *Calcio: A History of Italian Football*, author John Foot explains why *totonero* appealed to so many in Italy, including the players:

> Totonero *offered far greater opportunity for fixers, and was especially appealing to seasoned professionals, eager to make their last tax-free sums before retirement.* Totonero *also meant that players could bet on matches that had already been fixed for footballing [soccer] reasons.*

A total of seven Serie A teams, twenty players, and two team officials were punished for their involvement in the *totonero* scandal. Milan team president Felice Colombo received the worst punishment, as he was banned from soccer for life. This meant that he could no longer have any involvement with any team in Italian soccer. Milan goalkeeper Enrico Albertosi was banned for four years and never played for the team again. His teammates Stefano Chiodi and Giorgio Morini were also punished and never returned to Milan.

DEALING WITH RELEGATION

AC Milan's team punishment was also very harsh. The team finished in third place in Serie A for the 1979–1980 season with 14 wins and 36 points. However, once investigations revealed that three players and their team president had been involved in the scandal, AC Milan was disqualified for the season. They were placed in the bottom third of Serie A and automatically relegated, or dropped down, to Serie B for the next season.

The penalties that AC Milan received as a result of their involvement with the scandal affected the team for several years. Inconsistent results and player injuries would force the team to bounce back and forth

Shown here are AC Milan players from the 1979–1980 season. Members of this team were disqualified from Serie A because of their involvement in the gambling scandal that season.

between Serie A and Serie B for four difficult seasons. Despite their struggles over these roller coaster four years, the team has not been relegated again as of late 2019.

CALCIOPOLI

In 2006, AC Milan found themselves involved in another match-fixing scandal. This one was called the Italian football scandal, or "Calciopoli." The police investigation was about suspected match-fixing during the 2004–2005 Serie A season.

Italian police revealed phone records that indicated team managers from several of the country's biggest soccer teams had been trying to fix the results of games. The managers were working with the groups that select referees for each game. The report said

TEAM VALUE

Once one of the most valuable soccer teams in Europe, AC Milan has seen its value decrease in recent years. This is largely because of the ownership issues. Forbes *is an American business magazine. Every year, it ranks professional sports teams based on factors like ticket sales and sales of jerseys, hats, and food at games. According to* Forbes *magazine in May 2019, the overall value of the team was about €520 million ($583 million) in 2019, down from €554 million ($612 million) in 2018. At their peak in 2012, AC Milan was valued at €895 million ($989 million). Today, the team gets money through other areas like sponsorship. Emirates Airlines is one sponsor. A sponsor is an organization or person who gives money to a team in exchange for something. In Emirates' case, they pay the team about €90 million ($100 million), and the airline's name appears on the front of AC Milan jerseys. Other major sponsors for AC Milan are sports clothing giant Puma, Avis rental cars, and Konami, the team's official video game partner.*

LIVERPOOL RIVALRY

AC Milan has been very successful in UEFA Champions League play, with 7 titles, trailing only Real Madrid's 13. They've made 11 appearances in the championship game, including 2 against Liverpool, a top English soccer team. The Champions League is an annual event that features the national club team champions from across Europe. It's considered the most important club tournament.

AC Milan's Kaká (*left*) gets tangled up with Liverpool's Dietmar Hamann (*right*) during the memorable UEFA Champions League final on May 25, 2005.

AC Milan faced Liverpool in the Champions League title game twice in a three-year span during the 2000s. Liverpool has been among the world's top teams for many years. Since the two teams can only meet in European competitions, the matches between these two powerhouses are very intense and highly anticipated by soccer fans around the world.

The 2005 final was played in Istanbul, Turkey. It is considered by many people to be one of the best Champions League final games ever. Milan stunned Liverpool by taking a 3–0 lead before halftime. However, Liverpool fought back, scoring three goals in six minutes in the second half, before defeating Milan 3–2 on penalty kicks.

Milan got their revenge on Liverpool two years later in 2007 with a 2–1 win in Greece to claim their seventh Champions League title. Not only was this Milan's last appearance in a Champions League final as of 2019, but the two teams have yet to play each other since. Liverpool won the Champions League title in 2019 and were runners-up in 2018. Soccer fans everywhere are eagerly awaiting the next chapter in this rivalry.

Happy AC Milan players gather together to celebrate the team's 18th Serie A scudetto on May 24, 2011, at San Siro Stadium.

5 LOOKING TO THE FUTURE

It's been more than 100 years since Herbert Kilpin and Alfred Edwards started the Milan Foot-Ball and Cricket Club. It's probably safe to say that neither man knew what kind of legendary team they were creating. The AC Milan name has become known for its powerful teams and championship history. Many of the world's greatest players have worn the red-and-black uniforms, and young people today have those same dreams.

However, AC Milan is more than an Italian soccer team. They're a global brand with many fans all over the world. The AC Milan Fan Club has supporter groups called supporters' clubs. These fan clubs are in some of the world's biggest cities. All season long, fans meet to watch games on television, cheering on their soccer heroes.

AC MILAN IN AMERICA

American fans got a rare, in-person look at the team in the summer of 2019. AC Milan played two games in the United States as part of the International Champions Cup. This tournament featured 18 of the world's most successful soccer teams. One game was played in Kansas City, Kansas, against Bayern Munich of Germany. The other took place against Portugal's Benfica at Gillette Stadium in Foxborough, Massachusetts, the home of the National Football League's New England Patriots. To have AC Milan playing games in the United States is a sign of their international popularity and a tribute to how successful they've been over the years.

AMONG THE WORLD'S BEST

Having won many championships in Europe and Italy, AC Milan has received numerous honors and awards over the years to recognize these tremendous achievements. When the FIFA Club of the Century award was presented in December 2000 to honor the greatest soccer club of the 20th century, AC Milan tied for ninth overall in voting, alongside River Plate from Argentina and Flamengo from Brazil.

In addition, in 1998, a German soccer magazine called *Kicker* polled several of soccer's leading figures, including former players and managers, to determine the greatest clubs of the 20th century. Based on the five Champions League titles, two UEFA Cups, and three UEFA Super Cups they had earned at that time, AC Milan finished third overall, trailing only Real Madrid from Spain and Ajax from Amsterdam.

AC Milan finished fourth overall when the International Federation of Football History & Statistics (IFFHS) released their list of the Top 200 European clubs of the 20th century.

In 2007, *World Soccer* magazine ranked AC Milan's 1989–1990 team as the fourth-best team of all time.

Captain Franco Baresi, seen here (*left*) in action in December 1989, was a key part of AC Milan's dominant 1989–1990 team that's been considered one of soccer's top teams.

They were the highest ranked club team in the poll, finishing behind three national teams.

LIFE AT THE MILANELLO

When they aren't at San Siro, AC Milan players train at their Milanello Sports Center. Milanello was built in 1963 and is located 25 miles (40 kilometers) from Milan. This large complex includes six full-sized soccer fields, a pine forest, and a lake. It looks more like a vacation resort than a place for soccer players to train!

The people that run AC Milan are constantly improving the facilities with the best training equipment possible, while also making it a comfortable place for the players to relax before games. There's even a quiet

The AC Milan training center is one of the best facilities in the soccer world. Here, Colombian soccer player Carlos Bacca arrives at the center for a press conference in 2018.

running path that winds through the forested area around the training fields to help players with their altitude training and injury recovery. The facilities are so impressive that the Italian national team has trained there to prepare for major international events.

STADIUM PLANS

San Siro has been AC Milan's home stadium since 1926, and they've shared it with Inter Milan since 1947. There has been talk of renovating it again or building a new stadium for almost 10 years. Considering the age and size of the 80,000-seat stadium, team officials believe it's now time to build a brand-new home for AC Milan.

Officials from both teams met with the local government in July 2019 to discuss their plans. They also talked to several well-known stadium architects to create a design for their potential new home. If there are no holdups along the way, the new stadium will be ready in 2022. "We'll have the most beautiful stadium in the world," AC Milan president Paolo Scaroni told reporters in March 2019. "We want Milan to have a great stadium and make Milan the capital of football."

If the plans go forward as expected, Milan and Inter will continue to share a stadium. The current San Siro would be demolished, and a new stadium with approximately 60,000 seats would be constructed nearby. Several news reports also said they would model it after the 60,000-seat MetLife Stadium in New Jersey, home of the NFL's New York Jets and New York Giants.

Just like the Juventus Stadium complex in Turin and many others in England, the new stadium would also include an entertainment district surrounding the building, with shops and restaurants to improve the fan experience on game days. Plans also include a 5,000-seat venue to host music concerts.

The new stadium would also become the likely home for the opening ceremonies of the 2026 Winter Olympics. Those games will be hosted jointly by the Italian cities of Milan and Cortina d'Ampezzo.

SPORT SHORT

The AC Milan Fan Club has groups in major cities like New York City, Toronto, and London.

THE YOUTH SECTOR

In addition to adding players from all over the world to the Serie A lineup, the AC Milan Youth Sector is a program for the organization to train and discover the best young local players. There are nine teams in the youth program based on the players' ages, ranging from under 8 years old to under 17 years old. The program is based at Vismara Sports Centre in Gratosoglio, a suburb of Milan.

Milan also has an elite under-19 team that plays in the Campionato Nazionale Primavera. This is a league that's run by Serie A and has been around since 1962.

Milan's youth program has been the starting point for many high-profile players over the years who have had professional success. Paolo Maldini, Franco Baresi, and Alessandro Costacurta were all part of the youth program and went on to win multiple Serie A and European titles together. The three men combined to make 1,636 Serie A appearances for Milan during their careers.

THE FUTURE OF AC MILAN

Some of AC Milan's best players in recent years were also graduates of the youth program, including goalie Gianluigi Donnarumma. Born on February 25, 1999, Donnarumma was the team's starting goalkeeper by age 20 and is considered to be Italy's next goalkeeping superstar.

Forward Patrick Cutrone and defender Davide Calabria are also graduates of the youth program, and both were given important roles on the Serie A team at

Goalkeeper Gianluigi Donnarumma makes a save during a Serie A game in 2018. Donnarumma started his career in the AC Milan youth program.

a young age. Cutrone was with the youth program from 2007 to 2017 and made his debut with Milan in 2017. Calabria trained with the youth program from 2006 to 2015 and played his first game in Serie A as a 19-year-old in 2015.

AC Milan is always looking ahead, but they've also gone back to their roots in recent years by bringing an icon like Paolo Maldini back into the organization. Maldini was born in Milan, played his youth soccer in Milan, and retired as a proud and much-loved member of AC Milan. It's moves like these that will once again make AC Milan a European soccer champion and the pride of Milan.

CHRONOLOGY

1899 Herbert Kilpin and Alfred Edwards form the Milan Foot-Ball and Cricket Club.

1901 Milan wins its first Italian League championship.

1908 Disagreement about players results in a split to form Inter Milan.

1919 The team changes its name to Milan Football Club.

1926 AC Milan moves to the new San Siro Stadium.

1947 Inter Milan begins sharing San Siro with AC Milan.

1951 AC Milan wins its first Serie A title and its fourth Italian championship.

1963 AC Milan becomes first Italian team to win the European Cup.

1969 AC Milan defeats Ajax 4–1 to win a second European Cup.

1986 Silvio Berlusconi buys the team and becomes its new president.

1988 Marco van Basten wins the first of his three Ballon d'Or awards.

1989 AC Milan wins European Cup by a 4–0 score over Steaua Bucharest.

1990 AC Milan defeats Benfica 1–0 to win its second consecutive European Cup.

1992 AC Milan goes undefeated in Serie A, with 22 wins and 12 ties.

1993 The team's 58-game undefeated streak ends with a loss to Juventus.

1994 AC Milan wins its third straight Serie A title.

1999 AC Milan celebrates its 100th anniversary.

2007 AC Milan defeats Liverpool to win its seventh Champions League title.

2009 Legendary defender Paolo Maldini retires from soccer.

2011 AC Milan wins its 17th Serie A scudetto.

2016 AC Milan defeats Juventus to win its seventh Supercoppa Italiana.

2018 Elliott Management Corporation takes over ownership of AC Milan; Paolo Maldini is hired to help the team.

2019 *Forbes* magazine lists AC Milan as number 18 in top soccer teams (by value) around the world. The team promotes Paolo Maldini to the role of technical director with the club.

GLOSSARY

altitude Height above sea level; at high altitudes, the air is thinner and more difficult to breathe.

Ballon d'Or The award presented each year to a soccer player thought to be the best in the world.

calcio The Italian word for soccer.

chairman The leader of an organization such as a soccer club.

club team A team that belongs to a soccer club, usually based in a city; a local team, not a national team.

Coppa Italia An annual tournament that features the top teams from all four levels of Italian soccer.

debut The first appearance.

derby The name for regular games played between two rivals based close to each other geographically.

dictator A leader of a government who controls all parts of the government, usually harshly.

disqualified To be ineligible for a prize because a rule was broken.

FIFA The Féderation Internationale de Football Association, soccer's governing body.

illegal Against the law.

manager Also referred to as the head coach; the person in charge of a soccer team.

match An organized sporting event, also commonly referred to as a game.

promote To move a team to a higher level because they've won or done well in a season.

relegate To bring a team down to a lower league from a higher league.

renovate To repair or improve a building or structure through construction.

retire To be finished or no longer working in a certain professional career.

scandal An event that is legally wrong that upsets a large group of people.

scudetto Italian for "little shield," this refers to the jersey badge worn by the reigning Serie A champions.

Serie A The top level in Italian professional soccer.

striker A player at the front of the field during games who often scores goals; also called a forward.

tournament A series of games where teams compete for one trophy.

FURTHER INFORMATION

BOOKS

Mandis, Steven G. *What Happened to Serie A?: The Rise, Fall and Signs of Revival.* Edinburgh, UK: Arena Sport, 2018.

Nieri, Robert. *The Lord of Milan.* San Francisco, CA: Blurb, 2019.

Pirlo, Andrea. *I Think Therefore I Play.* United Kingdom: BackPage Press, 2015.

The Soccer Book, fourth ed. New York, NY: DK Publishing, 2018.

Whiting, Jim. *AC Milan.* Soccer Stars. Mankato, MN: Creative Company, 2017.

WEBSITES

AC Milan Official Website

www.acmilan.com/en

The team's official website features team news, game reports, photos, and ticket and merchandise sales.

Bleacher Report: AC Milan

bleacherreport.com/ac-milan

All the latest news and social media coverage about AC Milan is featured here.

ESPN: Serie A

www.espn.com/soccer/league/_/name/ita.1

Here you can find complete reporting of Italy's Serie A league, including team schedules and game recaps.

Forza Italian Football

forzaitalianfootball.com

Find in-depth coverage of all aspects of Italian soccer, including historical videos and travel guides, at this website.

UEFA

www.uefa.com

Learn more about the UEFA organization and its Champions League competition.

VIDEOS

AC Milan: One Century of Emotions

This film, which can be viewed on DVD, offers a historical look at how AC Milan has become one of the world's most powerful soccer teams.

AC Milan YouTube Channel

www.youtube.com/user/milanchannel

The team's official YouTube page features exclusive interviews, player features, and game highlights.

The Lord of Milan

This award-winning documentary, which can be viewed on DVD, profiles the fascinating life of Herbert Kilpin, the founder of AC Milan.

SELECTED BIBLIOGRAPHY

Bagchi, Rob. "The Rise and Fall of AC Milan and Inter: Why Both Clubs Must Ditch Imperious Self-Regard and Accept the Old Days Are Gone." *Telegraph*, October 20, 2016. www.telegraph.co.uk/football/2016/10/20/the-rise-and-fall-of-ac-milan-and-inter---why-both-clubs-must-di.

Cova, Ernesto. "Top 10 Best Players in AC Milan History." Fadeaway World, January 29, 2019. fadeawayworld.net/2019/01/29/top-10-best-players-in-ac-milan-history.

Cripps, Simon. "Gunnar Nordahl: The First Great Calcio Import." These Football Times, September 15, 2012. thesefootballtimes.co/2012/09/15/gunnar-nordahl-the-first-great-italian-import.

Hall, Richard. "Milan: Serie A Alternative Club Guide." *Guardian*, September 12, 2014. www.theguardian.com/football/the-gentleman-ultra/2014/sep/12/ac-milan-serie-a-alternative-club-guide.

Keogh, Frank. "Why It was the Greatest Cup Final." BBC Sport, May 26, 2005. news.bbc.co.uk/sport2/hi/football/4582357.stm.

Lawrence, Amy. "Maldini the One and Only Bows Out." *Guardian*, May 22, 2009. www.theguardian.com/football/blog/2009/may/22/paolo-maldini-ac-milan-retirement.

Newman, Blair. "The Highs and Lows of Silvio Berlusconi's AC Milan Reign." Bleacher Report, August 19, 2016. bleacherreport.com/articles/2658490-the-highs-and-lows-of-silvio-berlusconis-ac-milan-reign.

Probert, Tom. "Inter v AC Milan: A Brief History of the Derby della Madonnina." Forza Italian Football, October 19, 2018. forzaitalianfootball.com/2018/10/inter-v-ac-milan-a-brief-history-of-the-derby-della-madonnina.

Sherman, Justin. "The Devil's Odyssey: How Silvio Berlusconi Turned AC Milan Into a Superpower." These Football Times, October 18, 2018. thesefootballtimes.co/2018/04/18/the-devils-odyssey-how-silvio-berlusconi-turned-ac-milan-into-a-superpower.

Sidle, Ryan. "Throwback to One of the Most Iconic Moments in Milan Derby History." Sport Bible, October 14, 2017. www.sportbible.com/football/rivalries-throwback-to-one-of-the-most-iconic-moments-in-milan-derby-history-20171014.

Stewart, Kieran. "Arrigo Sacchi: The Prophet of Fusignano." The Versed, April 13, 2017. www.theversed.com/47510/arrigo-sacchi-the-prophet-of-fusignano/#.vSP0JWOA0E.

Townsend, Jon. "Marco van Basten: An Undisputed Legend Despite a Premature End." These Football Times, June 25, 2015. thesefootballtimes.co/2015/06/25/marco-van-basten-an-undisputed-legend.

Vasisht, Prateek. "Why AC Milan Remains the Greatest Club Side Ever." Total Football. Accessed March 20, 2019. medium.com/totalfootball/why-ac-milan-remains-the-greatest-club-side-ever-assembled-64ef27473d19.

Warren, Dan. "The Worst Scandal of Them All." BBC Sport, July 25, 2006. news.bbc.co.uk/sport2/hi/football/europe/5215260.stm.

INDEX

A

AC Milan Women, 31
altitude, 50

B

Ballon d'Or, 29–30, 32
Berlusconi, Silvio, 23, 25, 42
boycott, 16

C

calcio, 8, 15, 36
Calciopoli scandal, 38, 40
chairman, 14
Champions League, 11, 23–24, 27–29, 32, 36, 40–41, 44–45, 48
club team, 8, 11, 23, 44, 49
Coppa Italia, 25, 27–28

D

debut, 31, 53
derby, 18, 22, 27, 41
dictator, 15
disqualified, 37

E

extra time, 7

F

fan card, 41–42
Fédération Internationale de Football Association (FIFA), 32, 48
forward, 19, 52

G

goalie, 5–7, 52
Gre-No-Li, 20–21

I

illegal, 36

J

jersey, 6–7, 10, 39

K

Kilpin, Herbert, 12–15, 47

L

Liedholm, Nils, 20–22

M

Maldini, Paolo, 23, 30, 32, 43, 52–53
manager, 23, 38, 48
match, 37, 45
match-fixing, 36, 38

Mussolini, Benito, 15

N

Nordahl, Gunnar, 16, 19–22

P

pitch, 5
promote, 11

R

relegate, 11, 37–38, 40
renovate, 50
retire, 30, 37, 53
Ronaldo, Cristiano, 29

S

San Siro, 8, 17–18, 22, 41, 46, 49–51
scandal, 35–38
scudetto, 9, 24, 27, 30, 32
Serie A, 8–11, 16, 18–19, 21–25, 27–32, 37–38, 40, 42, 52–53
Serie B, 9–10, 37–38, 40
shootout, 7
soccer vs. football, 7
stadium, 17–18, 41–42, 48, 50–51
striker, 19, 29

T

tifosi, 41
Torino, 13
tournament, 11, 23–24, 29, 44, 47
Turin, 13, 51

U

UEFA Cup, 48
UEFA Super Cup, 24, 48
ultras, 40–41
Union of European Football Associations (UEFA), 11, 23–24, 31, 41, 44, 48
United States, fans in, 47–48

W

World War II, 15, 19

ABOUT THE AUTHOR

Kevin Snow is a Canadian-born sports and lifestyle freelance writer who has lived in Buffalo, New York, since 2000. Snow's professional career spans more than 25 years and includes 7 years in various editorial roles with *TV Guide Canada*, along with 10 seasons in public relations and marketing with the NHL's Buffalo Sabres. Snow has written for a variety of print and digital platforms in recent years, and he has also been a contributor to the Associated Press, Canadian Press, and NHL.com. Snow credits his success to the support provided to him by his wife, Christine, and daughter, Alexandra.